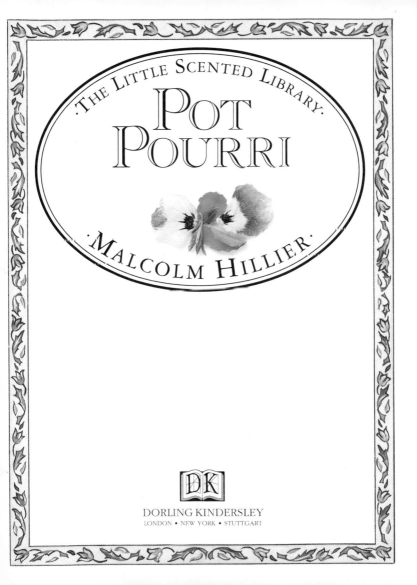

·THE LITTLE SCENTED LIBRARY·

POT POURRI

·MALCOLM HILLIER·

DK

DORLING KINDERSLEY
LONDON • NEW YORK • STUTTGART

DK

A DORLING KINDERSLEY BOOK

•

SERIES EDITORS HEATHER DEWHURST, MARY LAMBERT
PROJECT EDITOR SUSAN THOMPSON
ART EDITOR CAROL McCLEEVE
MANAGING EDITOR JANE LAING
SENIOR ART EDITOR DAVID ROBINSON
PRODUCTION MERYL SILBERT
PHOTOGRAPHY MATTHEW WARD

•

FIRST PUBLISHED IN GREAT BRITAIN IN 1991
BY DORLING KINDERSLEY LIMITED,
9 HENRIETTA STREET, LONDON WC2E 8PS

•

•

A CIP CATALOGUE RECORD FOR THIS BOOK IS AVAILABLE FROM THE BRITISH LIBRARY

•

ISBN 0-86318-559-2

•

COMPUTER PAGE MAKE-UP BY THE COOLING BROWN PARTNERSHIP
REPRODUCED BY COLOURSCAN, SINGAPORE
PRINTED IN HONG KONG

2

CONTENTS

3

INTRODUCTION

POT POURRI IS A FRAGRANT MIX of flower petals, herbs, spices, resins and essential oils, and has been used to perfume rooms and clothes since the times of the ancient Egyptians. Pot pourri is French for "rotten pot" and this refers to the moist method of preparation in which fragrant petals are fermented with salt before other scented materials are added for curing. Pot pourri can also be made by the simple method of mixing and curing all the dry ingredients together.

Many pot-pourri mixes have as their base either rose petals or lavender, but there are a host of other perfumed ingredients that can be used, including spring mimosa, narcissus, lily-of-the-valley and lilac, and summer peonies, pinks, jasmine and honeysuckle. Scented leaves lend a subtle aroma to pot pourri, while spices add an exotic piquancy. Each recipe needs a special fixative, such as orris root, tonka, or gum benzoin, to hold its fragile perfume secure and make it last.

The scents of pot pourris should never be too strong, just subtle enough to give the rooms in your home a hint of a delicious flowery fragrance that will appeal to everyone.

FLOWERS

FRAGRANT ROSE PETALS and lavender are the flowers most widely used in the making of pot pourri, but other kinds of commonly grown fragrant flowers and leaves can add their own particular perfumes, whether sweet or more reminiscent of the musky smells of the Orient, to your chosen mixes.

Rosemary has a sharp, woody, aromatic scent.

Stock has a heady and spicy, almost oriental perfume.

Lily-of-the-valley is a sweet and distinctive-smelling spring flower.

Freesia has a sweet scent.

Roses have the best of all perfumes.

Sweet pea has a pure perfume.

Lavender has an aromatic scent.

Lilies are extremely spicy.

Tobacco plant has a nutmeg scent.

Star jasmine has a stong, sweet scent.

Marigold has a sharp smell.

Pinks have an clove perfume.

Tuberose has a rich, heavy scent.

Mock orange has a heady fragrance.

Peonies have a buttery scent.

SPICES & FIXATIVES

*M*ANY POT-POURRI MIXES include some spices, and their warm, musky scents add depth to the fragrance of the mix. Fixatives, too, are an important ingredient in pot pourri. They absorb and hold the perfume of flower petals, which can be quite fleeting. The most commonly used fixative is ground orris root, which has a scent of violets. But there are many other fixatives you can use, most of which are aromatic and add to the bouquet of a pot pourri, such as frankincense, gum benzoin, oakmoss and tonka beans. Combine these with fragrant petals, herbs, and scented oils to make your own pot pourris.

Star anise smells of liquorice.

Citrus peel adds a sharp, piquant tang.

Lavender's newly opened flowers have the strongest scent.

Tonka beans are vanilla-scented and are used to scent tobacco.

Gum benzoin is a tree resin.

Frankincense or olibanum resin is the incense burnt in churches.

Oakmoss has a woody smell.

Cinnamon is finely ground to make a fixative. It combines well with most scented flowers.

Juniper berries have a pine smell when crushed.

Ginger root can be ground or sliced for a spicy scent.

Bay leaves are extremely aromatic.

Chamomile flowers have a tangy scent.

Hawthorn has a sharp smell when crushed.

Cedar cone segments have a strong woody smell.

Vanilla has a lightly spiced, caramel scent.

Cloves can be used for citrus pomanders.

Orris root has a strong, violet scent.

CHOOSING CONTAINERS

POTS WITH COVERS OR PERFORATED COVERS were used for pot pourris in the eighteenth and nineteenth centuries, when their scents were much lighter than our present ones and had to be preserved.

Nowadays, we can use almost any container that is not too shallow.

LIDDED DISH
*An eighteenth-
century dish
(right) with a cover
that helps to preserve
perfume.*

Were I so tall to reach the Pole,
Or grasp Creation with my span,
I must be measur'd by my soul,
The mind's the standard of the man.

GLAZED POTS
*The vase (top) and
two bowls (above),
made by the author,
are interesting colours
for pot pourris.*

ORIENTAL BOWL
This beautiful Chinese bowl would make the ideal vessel for a pot-pourri mix containing yellow, blue and orange flowers.

TOBACCO JAR
A lead tobacco jar makes an unusual covered container for pot pourri.

STRIKING CONTAINERS
The black and silver covered box (above) was made to contain spices. The contemporary pressed ceramic bowl (right) would be ideal for a blue and pink pot-pourri mix.

DRY POT POURRI

O MAKE A DRY POT POURRI, mix together dried, fragrant petals, leaves and seeds with a fixative, such as ground orris root, and essential oils. The quantities of each of the ingredients will vary according to the individual recipes. Place the mixture in a jar, then seal it and store in a dry place at room temperature for about six to eight weeks. Shake the pot pourri every day to ensure the ingredients are thoroughly combined.

Lavender

Dried marigolds

Dried rose petals

Cinnamon sticks

Dried helichrysum

Dried mint adds a piquancy to the mix.

Bergamot oil

Ground orris root has a sweet violet scent.

Lavender oil

BASIC DRY POT POURRI

Rose petals are the usual basis for dry pot pourris, but any fragrant petals are suitable. This basic garden mix does not need too many petals of any one flower.

SIMPLE MIX

Mix 250 ml (8 fl oz) each of dried roses, dried marigolds, dried peonies, and dried lavender. Add 125 ml (4 fl oz) dried helichrysum, and 1 tablespoon each of ground cinnamon, dried mint, and ground orris root. Finally mix in 4 drops each of bergamot and lavender oil.

EXOTIC MIXES

*I*T IS FUN TO EXPERIMENT with making unusual pot pourris. Most absorbent materials, such as moss, fruit, coral and seed heads, can be used in a mix, as long as there is a fixative in the pot pourri to soak up the scents. Try using scents that are non-floral. Clear glass can be an exciting vessel for displaying pot pourri as both the top and the sides of the mixture are visible, enabling you to build decorative patterns.

FRUITY MIX

This glass cube with its stripes of dried flowers, moss and fruits is filled with a fruity mix consisting of 250 ml (8 fl oz) each of lemon peel, lime peel, and lemon geranium leaves, 1 ground tonka bean, and 4 drops each of apricot oil and lemon oil.

OAKMOSS MIX

This rock pool pot pourri (opposite) consists of 750 ml (28 fl oz) oakmoss, 250 ml (8 fl oz) each of vetiver and blue delphinium flowers, and 4 drops of sandalwood oil, and is decorated with shells, coral, lotus, love-in-a-mist seed heads and blue delphinium flowers.

FLORAL MIXES

*D*ECORATE THE SURFACES of your pot pourri with dried flowers, both to enhance the appearance of the finished mix and to relate it to the colours of the bowl you use for your pot pourri.

LAVENDER & ROSE MIX

A large, floral Chinese bowl is filled with a mix of 2¹/₂ litres (5 pt) lavender flowers, 250 ml (8 fl oz) each of ground rosemary and rose buds, 500 ml (1 pt) lemon balm, 25 g (1 oz) gum benzoin, and 10 drops of lavender oil. The top is decorated with small posies of dried flowers tied with raffia.

MARIGOLD MIX

A tangy marigold pot pourri in an English delft bowl contains 500 ml (1 pt) marigolds, 250 ml (8 fl oz) each of hops and sandalwood shavings, and 1 tablespoon each of ground bay leaves and ground nutmeg. The top is decorated with dried marigolds, larkspur, hops, and bay leaves.

HEATHER & SAGE MIX

This small, painted Chinese bowl is filled with 750 ml (28 fl oz) heather flowers, 2 tablespoons each of ground marjoram and ground sage, 1 tablespoon of ground cinnamon, and 3 drops of balsam oil. It is decorated on top with some attractive dried peonies and Jerusalem sage to contrast strongly with the deep blue colour of the bowl.

HERB & SPICE MIXES

PECIAL CONTAINERS ARE AN INTEGRAL part of striking pot pourris, and relating the two elements is both interesting and fun to do. Colour, form, and texture need to be considered carefully. Choose containers that either complement or contrast with the colour scheme of the pot pourri, or that accentuate the texture of the mix. Whilst the basis of the pot pourri is most important, it is usually the final decoration – the dried flowers, seeds, and leaves, which need not be scented – that makes it so distinctive.

MARIGOLD & MINT MIX

*Mix 750 ml (28 fl oz) marigolds, 250 ml (8 fl oz)
each of peppermint leaves and tansy flowers, 1
tablespoon ground orris root, and 5 drops of
peppermint oil for a striking pot pourri (opposite).*

WOODY MIX

*This basket (below) is
crammed with spices,
seeds, and
scented oils.*

19

MOIST POT POURRI

HE MOIST METHOD of producing a pot pourri is very simple. Layer partially dried, fragrant petals with coarse salt and stir daily. You can add more petals as they are ready. The final mix must ferment for at least ten days. Add the remainder of the ingredients, seal, and leave for six to eight weeks, shaking daily.

Rose petals

Lime

Dill weed

Lemon verbena leaves

Pink

Brown sugar

Rose oil

Cloves

Gum benzoin

Coarse salt

Carnation oil

ROSE & PINK MIX

Dry 1¹/₂ litres (3 pt) rose and pink petals and 500 ml (1 pt) lemon verbena on newspaper or cheesecloth for two or three days. Layer them with 375 ml (12 fl oz) coarse salt in a sealed jar and stir each day for ten days. Mix in 3 tablespoons each of dried lime peel and dried dill, 1 tablespoon of cloves, 2 tablespoons each of brown sugar and gum benzoin, and 4 drops each of rose and carnation oils. Store for six to eight weeks, shaking daily.

COUNTRY MIXES

THINKING OF NEW WAYS to use pot pourri is a challenge. Country baskets, with their sympathetic colours and textures, make attractive containers for pot pourri. Here the rim of the basket has been decorated with bunches of herbs and flowers, attached with mossing wire and a glue gun. The basket holds a similar pot-pourri mix.

22

SUMMER FLOWER MIX

Mix together 750 ml (28 fl oz) rose petals, 750 ml (28 fl oz) peony petals, 500 ml (1 pt) clove pinks, 250 ml (8 fl oz) lavender, 250 ml (8 fl oz) each of rosemary, bay, and marjoram leaves, 2 tablespoons each of sage and cloves, 3 crushed tonka beans, and 750 ml (28 fl oz) coarse salt.

COLOURFUL MIXES

BOWLS OF POT POURRI can be as beautiful as flower arrangements. Display them on a side or low table, in living rooms or bedrooms. It is best to place them in low light as bright sunshine will soon make them fade.

SPRING FLOWER MIX
A delicate spring mix of 1.25 litres (40 fl oz) mixed fragrant narcissus, lilac, lily-of-the-valley, mimosa, jasmine, pansies, and wallflowers, 250 ml (8 fl oz) coarse salt, 2 tablespoons of ground orris root, and 4 drops of lily-of-the-valley oil.

RICH ROSE MIX

A rich, moist pot pourri composed of 1 litre (2 pt) fragrant red rose petals, 500 ml (1 pt) clove pinks, 125 ml (4 fl oz) tuberose, 250 ml (8 fl oz) coarse salt, 2 tablespoons each of ground cloves, ground ginger, and frankincense, and 4 drops of gardenia oil sits in a bowl edged with striking, dried tropical leaves.

MOIST CLOVER MIX

A basket edged with lavender is filled with a moist mix of 250 ml (8 fl oz) clover, 500 ml (1 pt) moss, 250 ml (8 fl oz) each of Spanish broom and bergamot leaves, 1 tablespoon of nutmeg, 250 ml (8 fl oz) coarse salt, 1 tablespoon of ground orris root, and 4 drops of honeysuckle oil.

DRIED FLOWERS

*P*OT POURRI COMBINES well with dried-flower arrangements. I often use pot pourri to cover and surround the dry foam in a container of dried flowers, as it adds so much fragrance. If the vase is made of clear glass, you have the added bonus of being able to see the pot pourri as well. To achieve this effect, carefully pack the pot pourri between the dry foam and the inner surfaces of the glass, building it up slowly and inserting some beautiful silica-gel dried flowers right next to the glass. To position these delicate flowers without actually creasing their petals, try using a long-bladed icing knife and keep checking their position in the vase to see how the finished pot-pourri mixture is looking.

SCENTED DRIED FLOWERS

A rectangular glass vase is a good shape for this informal arrangement of dried peonies, roses, larkspur, campion, helichrysum, wheat, thistles, and eucalyptus. I attached dry foam to the base of the vase, leaving a 1 cm (³/4 in) gap around all the sides, which I filled with a fragrant rose pot pourri and some decorative dried flowers.

USING CANDLES

*Y*ou can make you own scented candles by melting candle wax, adding one or more essential oils with a few drops of food colouring, and then moulding them in a tin with a hole at the bottom through which a waxed wick has been threaded. Or you can choose from a wide range of scented candles available in shops and use one or more in a display that is itself scented. Here a bark-covered bowl is packed with dry foam into which three squat, honey-scented candles are anchored, before other decorations are added. This is an ideal arrangement for a Christmas table.

FESTIVE CANDLES

The centre of this festive arrangement is covered with dried moss and cones, which are impregnated with pine oil and ground cinnamon. Bundles of cinnamon sticks, blue spruce, and tiny, dried, red roses are wired into position among the bark, away from the candles. For safety's sake, do not leave the lit candles unattended and do not allow them to burn too low.

29

MAKING A PILLOW

*M*ANY HERBS AND FLOWERS can be used to stuff pillows and cushions. As well as perfuming a room, they can have the added benefit of helping you sleep. Hops, woodruff, and rosemary are known for their sleep-inducing properties.

MAKING A SLEEP PILLOW

1 Either make or buy a pillow and stuff it with a mixture of wadding and 250 ml (8 fl oz) scented pot pourri.

2 Cut a length of material to cover the pillow, edge the long sides with lace, and sew the short sides together to make a cylinder. Attach ribbon ties to the open sides.

3 Slip the cover over the pillow, and keep it in place by tying the ribbons together into secure and attractive bows.

SOOTHING SCENTS
Use any fragrant combinations of soothing herbs and flowers, such as marjoram, thyme, chamomile, roses, or lavender, together with spices and a fixative, such as ground orris root, as stuffing for your pillows and cushions. The perfume should not be too strong.

HERB CUSHIONS

CUSHIONS AND PILLOWS with a delicately scented filling of pot pourri and herbs provide another way of scenting rooms. It is important that the cushions have just a hint of fragrance and are not too strongly scented. The desired effect is to make one feel relaxed in the living room, and soothed in the bedroom for a good night's sleep.

SWEET DREAMS

This sleep pillow is filled with 250 ml (8 fl oz) each of lemon thyme and lavender, 500 ml (1 pt) lemon verbena, and 2 drops of lavender oil.

ROSE-SCENTED CHINTZ

This large, glazed chintz cushion holds a pot-pourri filling consisting of 750 ml (28 fl oz) fragrant rose petals, the dried, grated peel of 2 lemons, 1 tablespoon of ground orris root, and 2 drops of lemon oil. If the perfume of the pot pourri mix begins to fade over time, simply add a few more drops of lemon oil to revive it.

HINT OF HERBS

This smaller chintz cushion has a herby mix of 500 ml (1 pt) mixed dried rosemary, peppermint, lemon balm, marjoram and basil, 125 ml (4 fl oz) oakmoss, and 3 drops of rosemary oil.

MAKING A SACHET

*S*ACHETS CONTAINING FRAGRANT flowers, herbs, and spices make beautiful presents and leave the most delicious scent when laid in drawers, especially between sheets and pillow cases. They are simple to make and their scent will last for up to a year.

MAKING A SACHET

1 Cut out two squares of fabric. With right sides together, stitch three sides and part of the fourth. Turn and fill the centre with pot pourri.

2 Stitch along the fourth edge to seal the sachet, then sew lace trimming around all the edges. Overlay this with a length of narrow ribbon in a complementary colour, leaving a short piece at one corner.

3 Sew the ribbon along both its edges, around all four sides of the sachet. Neaten the corners as you go, so that the ribbon lies flat. To finish, tie the two ends of the ribbon into a neat, decorative bow.

SACHET FILLINGS

Here are some fragrant fillings for your sachets: pinks, frankincense, and cloves; peonies, lemon balm, grated lemon, and coriander; and violets, roses, nutmeg, and ground orris root.

SCENTED SACHETS

*P*LACE FRAGRANT SACHETS in linen cupboards or drawers so they can lend their sweetness to clothes and linens. Many herbs, such as cotton lavender, rosemary, and southernwood, make good moth-repellents, and they smell much sweeter than chemical moth balls. Place these herby sachets among your woollens.

HANGING SACHETS
Two pouches that can be hung from a hook contain 250 ml (8 fl oz) each of rose petals and mint, and 1 tablespoon of ground cloves.

DUAL-PURPOSE SACHET

This sachet can be hung in a cupboard or placed flat in a drawer to deter moths. It is filled with a mix of 250 ml (8 fl oz) each of southernwood, rosemary, and lemon verbena, and 1 ground tonka bean.

MINIATURE CUSHION

This sachet is filled with scented rose petals and dried lavender, and 2 drops of lavender oil.

DRAWER SACHET

This flat sachet is filled with 250 ml (8 fl oz) fragrant rose petals, and 125 ml (4 fl oz) each of rose geranium leaves, oakmoss, and vetiver.

POMANDERS

*P*OMANDERS, from the French *pomme d'ambre*, were originally fragrant beads of ambergris strung on a necklace or placed in a perforated gold, silver, or wooden ball to be worn hanging from a necklace, bracelet, or belt. Today, pomanders are usually perforated ceramic spheres filled with pot pourri, or citrus fruits closely covered with cloves and fixed with orris root and other spices.

ANTIQUE POMANDER
This 19th-century pomander has been carved and pierced from a nut. It unscrews into two halves to hold either beads of ambergris or a fragrant pot pourri.

Cloves

Kumquats

Ground orris root

Lime

CITRUS POMANDER
Completely cover an orange or lemon with cloves, then roll it in ground orris root and store in a paper bag for several weeks until it is dry.

ROSE POMANDER

*A muslin bag tightly
packed with rose pot
pourri is covered
with little dried
roses, to form a
decorative and
perfumed,
hanging sphere.*

SCENTED FRUIT BASKET

*A group of citrus pomanders are
displayed in a basket of pot
pourri made from mixed
flower petals fragrant
with nutmegs,
cloves, coriander,
cinnamon, and
myrrh.*

INDEX

ACKNOWLEDGMENTS

The author *would like to thank the following people
for their help:* MAY CRISTEA, PETER DAY, MRS P FRANKLYN,
SARAH FRANKLYN, M HANDFORD ANTIQUES, JENNY RAWORTH,
and QUENTIN ROAKE.

Dorling Kindersley *would like to thank* STEVE DOBSON
for his help with photography.

Border illustrations *by Dorothy Tucker.*